D0341672

# Merry Christmas, My Dear Friend

Copyright © 2016 by Suzy Toronto.

All rights reserved. No part of this publication may be reproduced, stored in a retrieval
system or transmitted in any form or by any means, electronic, mechanical, photocopying,
recording or otherwise, without the written permission of the publisher.

ISBN: 978-1-59842-998-5

**Wonderful Wacky Women.**
Inspiring•Uplifting•Empowering

is a trademark of Suzy and Al Toronto. Used under license.

▉ and Blue Mountain Press are registered in U.S. Patent and Trademark Office.
Certain trademarks are used under license.

Printed in China.
First Printing: 2016

♲ This book is printed on recycled paper.

This book is printed on paper that has been specially produced to be acid free (neutral pH)
and contains no groundwood or unbleached pulp. It conforms with the requirements of the
American National Standards Institute, Inc., so as to ensure that this book will last and be
enjoyed by future generations.

# Blue Mountain Arts, Inc.
P.O. Box 4549, Boulder, Colorado 80306

# Merry Christmas, My Dear Friend

Suzy Toronto

**Blue Mountain Press**™
Boulder, Colorado

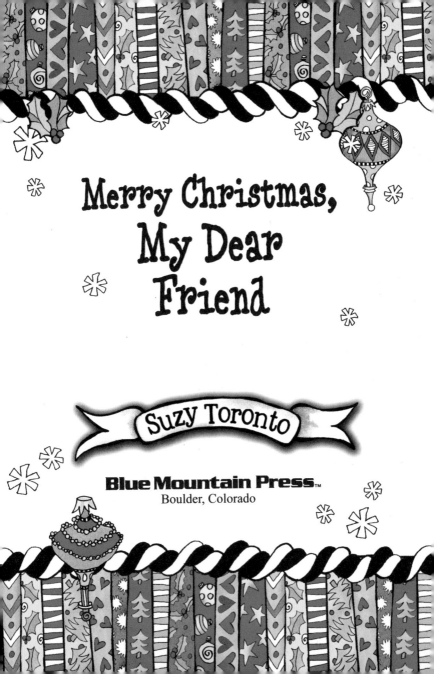

# Merry Christmas, My Dear Friend

As the Christmas season comes upon us, it reminds me how blessed I am to have you in my life. As friends, we've been through so much together. And each year brings us even closer as our bond grows and grows.

People often joke and say silly things like,
"I have to keep you as my friend…
you know too much!" as if that's a bad thing.
But over the years, the more we learn and share,
the more relaxed we are with each other.
I can't even begin to describe how comforting it is
to be able to talk to you about anything and not
have to preface it with a long, drawn-out history.
You already know all the details and contingencies.
We are at the point where one of us can
start a thought and the other will finish it.
I am grateful for that kind of intimacy…
that kind of friendship.
It's a rare and precious thing.

So as we celebrate yet another Christmas,
I also celebrate another year
of having you in my life.
I have received the greatest gift of all…
your love, acceptance,
and unending friendship.

© Suzy Toronto

# Having you as a friend is like Christmas every day!

As much as I love being around my family at Christmas, I'm so glad to have a girlfriend like you.

With all the craziness and chaos
the holiday season brings,
it's wonderful knowing
you're always there.
Whether we talk about what to cook
or what to wear to some party,
our conversations ground me.
They bring a sense of sanity to my life
that can otherwise be quite frenetic.
When all the presents
have been exchanged
and the Christmas parties are over,
I cherish the memories
and time spent together with you.
I will forever appreciate
the relationship we have
shared over the years.
It's the best gift you ever gave me.

Having you for a friend
truly is like Christmas every day.

©Suzy Toronto

If there had been
three wise women,
they would have arrived
three days early,
swept the stable,
gathered fresh linens,
and had a hot meal ready and waiting
when the Christ child arrived.

Yet they come today
bearing three priceless gifts…
an abundance of heartfelt love,
boundless fits of irrepressible laughter,
and friendship that will
forever stand the test of time.

© Suzy Toronto

# I Love Who I Am When I Am with You

When I am around you,
not only can I be
my crazy, wacky self,
but you make me
want to be
my best crazy,
wacky self.

With you by my side,
I'm willing to take a chance,
because in the end,
I know you've always got my back.

You are the strength in our relationship —
the anchor and the beacon. You keep me
grounded and at the same time hand me
a set of wings and encourage me to fly.
You are a light in my life that, frankly,
I can't imagine ever being without.

But the bottom line is this:
I love who I am when I am around you.
I feel blessed beyond words
that not only do I call you my friend,
but in the end,
you call me your friend too.

Thank you for being
such a bright light in my life!

©Suzy Toronto

# Thoughts of Our Friendship Make My Heart Tingle

Right from the start, I knew our friendship was unique.

We are like yin and yang,
witty and wacky,
yet we fit together so perfectly,
creating an unbreakable bond.
The individual challenges we've faced
have drawn our hearts closer
as we took turns pushing each other
into the light, helping to keep
the other's priorities and perspectives.
Most important of all,
we've kept our sense of humor,
always ready with a laugh or a smile
through life's greatest lessons.
What we have is unique indeed…
a meeting of the minds
that when we're together makes us strong.

Together… our hearts are empowered.
Together… life is a wonderful, wacky adventure,
and having you by my side
makes all the difference.

© Suzy Toronto

Anyone Who Says She
Doesn't Need a Girlfriend
Just Hasn't Found
a Good One Yet

What a blessing it is to be surrounded by
the most amazing women who are my friends!
I just can't bear the thought of
picking up the phone
and not having one of them
to talk to, cry to, and visit with.
They are my biggest critics,
favorite sounding boards,
and personal cheerleading squad
all rolled into one.

My world is infinitely more exciting, fun,
wacky, peaceful, interesting, and real
simply because of girlfriends like you.
Having you in my life
is a blessing I will never
take for granted,
a sisterhood
that lasts forever.

© Suzy Toronto

I've decided to simplify my life
and only focus on those things
that are most important
in the grand scheme of life,
the universe, and everything else.
I have refined my quest and narrowed my vision
to two important, nonnegotiable things:
 1. I want peace on earth.
    (Great answer just in case I get
      a chance to be in a beauty pageant
        and maybe win that longed-for tiara.)
 2. I want a really cute pair of shoes.
    Yes, I am a woman on a mission!
      I am in search of (breathe)…
    THE most magnificently wonderful,
      fabulously adorable,
    irresistibly cute little ole pair of shoes
      on the face of the earth!
        So please, dear Santa,
          let every gift under the tree
          be a shoebox!

Everyone knows all too well
that behind every successful man
is a really great woman.
And the one behind the big jolly man
in the bright red suit is no exception.
After all, it's her job to tend to
all the important stuff...
like keeping him organized and fed,
which are obviously no small tasks!
She wouldn't dare leave
the "Naughty and Nice List" up to him...
he'd get them all mixed up.
If it wasn't for her, little Susie
would end up with a baseball mitt
and Jimmy would get
the baby doll that cuddles and coos.
And for all this work and sacrifice,
who gets the credit?
The big fat guy who'd lose his beard
if it weren't stuck to his chin!

Yes, everyone knows that behind
every big jolly guy
is a wild, wacky,
and truly wonderful woman.

# ...the pounds would just melt away!

Whoever thought of dieting through the holidays
just didn't "get it."
Memories of Christmas have always included
special treats and yummy meals.
As the holidays approach,
we love to nibble on gooey, luscious fudge
and those little, buttery snowball cookies.
And seriously, how could anyone possibly say "no"
to that succulent turkey dinner
with all the trimmings
that begs us to take one more bite?
Turning it down just wouldn't be right.

But come January, the scale reminds us that
we might have enjoyed all those goodies
just a little bit too much.
That's when we all wish
we were simply made of snow.
For then, in the spring,
the pounds would just melt away!

It's So Wonderful to Have
a Wacky Friend
like
You

I feel so blessed to
have you in my life.
We are alike in
so many ways,
yet different in
so many others.
It seems to give a
wonderful balance
to the sometimes
wild and wacky
lives we lead.

© Suzy Toronto

Whether we are giggling, whining, or crying,
we always seem to have a good time doing it.
We have more fun than anyone
should be allowed to, and in the end,
we validate that maybe, just maybe,
our wacky lives are normal after all.

But what I really love about us are our differences.
You are strong when I am not,
levelheaded when I'm feeling a bit off balance,
and you lift me up when I think I can't go on.

And then, the icing on the cake...
you put up with the very *worst* in me
because, deep down inside, you know
the *best* in me is worth the hassle!

What a match we make!
Two wild, wacky, wonderful women
together riding in the front seat
of the roller coaster of life...
and having the time of our lives.

And I can't think of anyone
I'd rather do it with.

She Who
Celebrates
All Year
Long

In February she's still listening to Bing Crosby
croon "White Christmas,"
and regardless of the season, "Silent Night"
is her lullaby for any baby she holds.

In midsummer her home reflects
the enchantment of the holidays,
for the outside is still illuminated
with the magic of little white twinkle lights,
despite the sultry heat.

By September she's dusted off
the Christmas movies and she's already
scouting the woods for the perfect tree.

Come November she's totally caught up
in the dreamlike wonder of the holiday season.
For you see, she *is* the Spirit of Christmas,
and she celebrates all year long.

©Suzy Toronto

At Christmastime, I am reminded how grateful I am to have you for a friend

Sometimes I wonder... what would it be like to have a friend who knows me inside and out — all the good, all the bad — and loves me anyway?

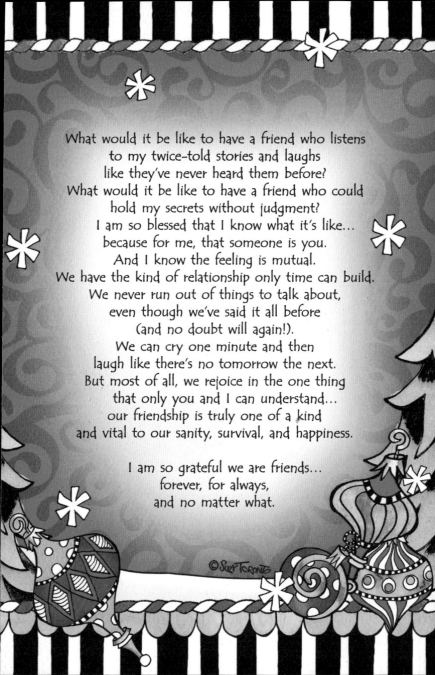

What would it be like to have a friend who listens
to my twice-told stories and laughs
like they've never heard them before?
What would it be like to have a friend who could
hold my secrets without judgment?
I am so blessed that I know what it's like...
because for me, that someone is you.
And I know the feeling is mutual.
We have the kind of relationship only time can build.
We never run out of things to talk about,
even though we've said it all before
(and no doubt will again!).
We can cry one minute and then
laugh like there's no tomorrow the next.
But most of all, we rejoice in the one thing
that only you and I can understand...
our friendship is truly one of a kind
and vital to our sanity, survival, and happiness.

I am so grateful we are friends...
forever, for always,
and no matter what.

© Suzy Toronto

The First Noel...
the Very
First Night

Two thousand years ago,
a child was born.
The angel sang, the shepherds came,
and the wise men followed the star.
They said He was the
Son of God,
the Prince of Peace.

But none of that mattered to Mary
that very first night.
As she gently cradled Him in her arms
and softly sang Him a sweet lullaby,
all she saw was her precious baby boy.
And for her, that was heaven enough.

As we enjoy this holiday season,
let's take a moment to ponder
the miracle of that
very first Christmas...
and the joy that this baby boy
has brought to us all.

© Suzy Toronto

Make Your
Christmas a
Work of
HeART

This year, vow to really *live*
Christmas with all your heart.
Design it with dreams and desires.
Plan it with power and purpose.
Color it with creativity and compassion,
and forge it with family and friends.
Envelop it with energy and enthusiasm,
and wrap it up with all the warmth
and wonder the season has to offer.
If that's not your thing,
paint it with laughter,
roll it in sequins and glitter,
and string it up
with a kajillion of those
little, sparkly twinkle lights.

Either way, you can't go wrong.
Just make sure
you do it all
with love.

©Suzy Toronto

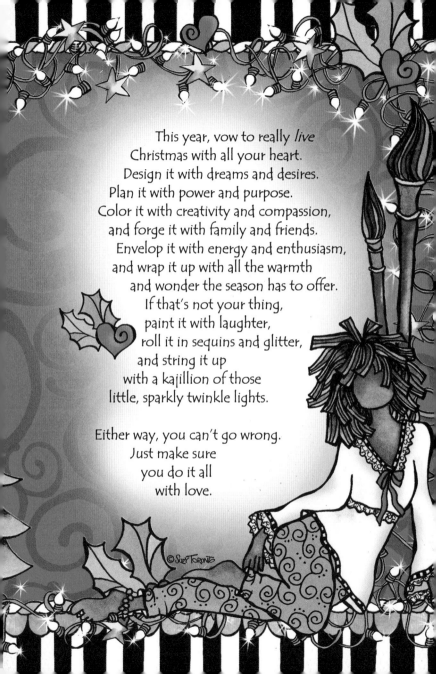

# I'm So Grateful God Allowed Our Paths to Cross

As our paths crossed,
we reached out and
grabbed each other,
refusing to ever let go...
two wacky women
clinging to each other
as if our lives depended on it.

God didn't create us with the same bloodline...
but He might as well have.
For you and I have mixed our diversity
into an eternal, sacred sisterhood
stronger than any natural bond.
We are sisters by choice...
not by chance.

How wonderful that you
get me and I get you.
We accept each other "as is"...
no apologies, no excuses, no judgments.
Whether laughing hysterically until we cry
or crying buckets of tears until we laugh,
you embrace all the goodness I have to offer,
and then, with a breath of kindness,
blow the rest away.
It's the way sisterhood should be.

I'm so grateful God brought us
two wacky women together...
two soul mates, two eternal spirits,
two forever friends.

© Suzy Toronto

# You're the kind of friend everyone wishes they had

I've pretty much decided that when it comes to being a friend, you have mastered the class. You have been such a cherished friend to me.

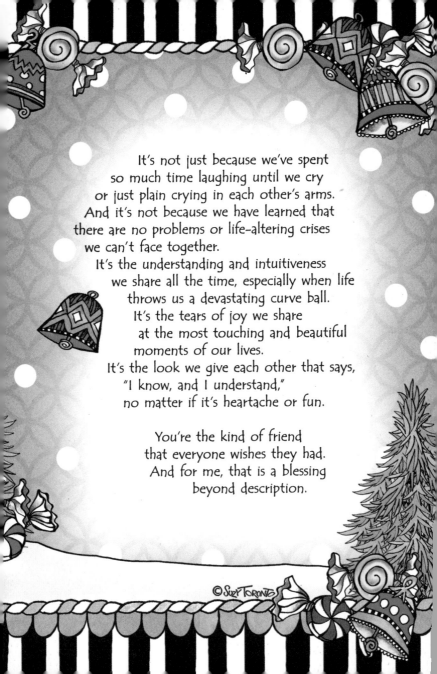

It's not just because we've spent
so much time laughing until we cry
or just plain crying in each other's arms.
And it's not because we have learned that
there are no problems or life-altering crises
we can't face together.
It's the understanding and intuitiveness
we share all the time, especially when life
throws us a devastating curve ball.
It's the tears of joy we share
at the most touching and beautiful
moments of our lives.
It's the look we give each other that says,
"I know, and I understand,"
no matter if it's heartache or fun.

You're the kind of friend
that everyone wishes they had.
And for me, that is a blessing
beyond description.

©Suzy Toronto

# You Are Surrounded by Christmas Angels

Having angels in your life is no big thing... it's a zillion little things. They comfort you when you're down and encourage you when you struggle. The best angels give you what you need, not what you want — even if that's a good swift kick!

Angels are better at cheering than jeering.
Their unseen powers of goodness are
all around you. Angels give you that tingle
you feel when you are surrounded by
love and faith. They help you to do what's
right, especially when it's not easy.
Visible angels are always encircling you,
masquerading as family, friends,
and even strangers who lend a
helping hand or offer a kind word.
Act on the faith that you are not alone, and
believe your angels will make everything all
right. There are angels surrounding
you this very moment... just believe.

© Suzy Toronto

# A Forever Friend like You Is a Christmas Blessing I Truly Cherish

Every so often, fate brings together two souls... kindred spirits whose paths have crossed in another time and place... and there is never a disconnect.

It is comforting beyond words to know
that no matter the time or distance,
the other is only a phone call away.
It's just a fact:
we would drop everything
for each other if needed.

And when we do connect,
we pick up right where we left off.
Our conversations begin and end mid-paragraph.
We both know where to start up again —
like we were never apart.
What a balm of comfort it is
to have you in my life!
It is a wonderful blessing to have
such a fabulous friend like you.

You and me...
two wonderful, wacky women.
Kindred spirits... forever friends,
connected heart to heart.

© Suzy Toronto

# About the Author

So this is me… I'm a tad wacky and just shy of crazy. I'm fiftysomething and live in the sleepy village of Tangerine, Florida, with my husband, Al, and a big, goofy dog named Lucy. And because life wasn't crazy enough, my eightysomething-year-old parents live with us too. (In my home, the nuts don't fall far from the tree!) I eat far too much chocolate, and I drink sparkling water by the gallon. I practice yoga, ride a little red scooter, and go to the beach every chance I get. I have five grown children and over a dozen grandkids who love me as much as I adore them. I teach them to dip their French fries in their chocolate shakes and to make up any old words to the tunes they like. But most of all, I teach them to never, ever color inside the lines. This is the Wild Wacky Wonderful life I lead, and I wouldn't have it any other way. Welcome to my world!